LITTLE BIG BOOKS

FASTEST THINGS

JONATHAN RUTLAND

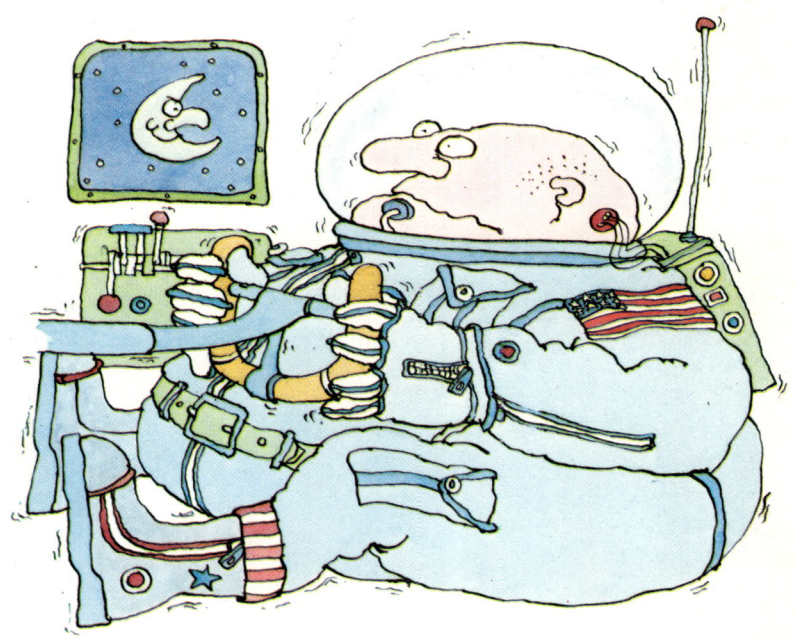

Editor: Trisha Pike   Designer: Jacky Cowdrey
Picture Researcher: Kathy Brandt

Purnell

1 MANPOWER

Above: Robert Lee Hayes is the fastest runner.

Below: Many people enjoy watching sporting events to see who can go the fastest.

Since 1963 Robert Lee Hayes, an American from Florida, has held the record for the world's fastest runner. During a short run he reached 44.88 kilometres per hour (k.p.h.). The fastest ice skater travelled a little faster at 47.36 k.p.h. The fastest roller skater is Italian and he travelled a little slower at 41.48 k.p.h.

The longer the race, the slower the average speed. The record for the 100 yard (91.44 metre) race is nine seconds—an average speed of 36.57 k.p.h. The fastest woman over

Walker 14 k.p.h.

Roller skater 41.48 k.p.h.

Swimmer 8.20 k.p.h.

the same distance took one second longer, and averaged almost 33 k.p.h. In the 1,000 metre race the record is just under 27 k.p.h., while in a race an hour long it is 21 k.p.h.

The fastest swimmer reached 8.20 k.p.h., while the fastest walkers can keep up 13 or 14 k.p.h. for two hours.

The fastest cyclist travelled at 226 k.p.h. But he was helped because he rode behind a car which had a large windshield fixed at the back—so the slipstream of the car helped to pull him along. The highest speed a cyclist has pedalled with no help at all is 76.92 k.p.h.

Above: Speed skating is an event in the Olympics. The fastest speed is 47.36 k.p.h. Cyclist 76.92 k.p.h.

Ice skater 47.36 k.p.h.

Runner 44.88 k.p.h.

2 DIVE AND SLIDE

Parachutes were invented to save lives. But today many people enjoy a sport called sky diving. They leap out of an aeroplane and dive through the sky without opening their parachutes—until they are about 700 metres from the ground. During the 'free fall' the diver drops thousands of metres.

You would think that a diver's speed would get faster and faster until he opens the parachute, but it does not. Try running into a very strong wind, and you will see why.

Below: Three sky divers hold hands to form a circle as they drop thousands of metres through the sky before opening their parachutes.

The air slows him down. After about a quarter of a minute he reaches a speed of nearly 300 k.p.h. From then on he falls at a steady speed. Even so, 300 k.p.h. is very fast—faster than any other sliding or diving sport. At great heights, where the air is much thinner, sky divers have fallen at 988 k.p.h.

On the famous Cresta Run in Switzerland one-man toboggans reach 135 k.p.h. The fastest speed on skis is almost 195 k.p.h.

In water skiing, when the skier is towed behind a speedboat, the record speed is 202 k.p.h.

Above: Water skiing started with riding on planks, now the fastest skier skims along at 202 k.p.h.

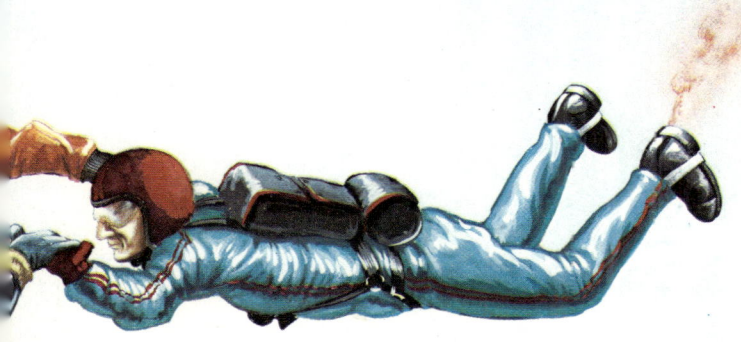

3 ANIMALS ON LAND

Some animals are good long-distance runners. Other animals are sprinters. Sprinters are strong enough to be able to run very fast over a short distance.

The world's fastest long distance runner is the Pronghorn antelope of the United States. It likes racing alongside cars. It can run happily for kilometre after kilometre at a steady 56 k.p.h. The cheetah is a sprinter and most people think it is the fastest land animal of all. Measuring the exact speed of any wild animal is difficult. Some people say they have timed cheetahs running at 145 k.p.h. But most people think that cheetahs' top speed is 104 k.p.h.

Most of the fastest animals are long-legged antelopes, gazelles and

Above: Cheetahs use their full speed on the grassy plains to chase antelopes.

Right: The Pronghorn likes to race beside moving cars.

deer. The British Red deer can run at 67 k.p.h. A smaller high-speed animal is the racing greyhound which can run at 67 k.p.h. The California jack rabbit runs at 64 k.p.h. The coyote, the jackal and the European rabbit all run at 56 k.p.h. Man comes low on the list with a top speed of about 45 k.p.h.

Left: The Sailfish is the fastest fish in the ocean.

4   SWIFTEST SEA CREATURES

Moving through water is much harder work than moving through air. This is because water is so much thicker. Yet the fastest fish, the Sailfish, travels faster than any land animal. The usual way of finding a sea creature's speed is to measure how quickly it pulls out the fishing line when it is firmly hooked. Once a Sailfish pulled out just over 91 metres of fishing line in three seconds. This showed that it was travelling at almost 110 k.p.h. and that is much faster than any submarine can travel.

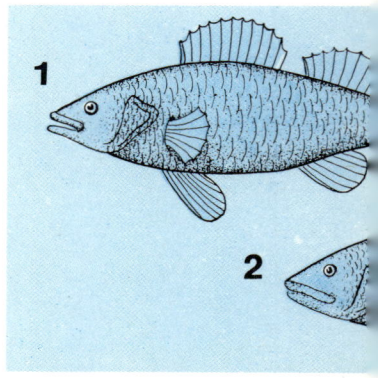

   All fast fish have bodies like slim torpedoes. They have powerful tails which are forked or shaped like half-moons. When moving at speed

Above: Marlins swim at 80 k.p.h. but this one did not manage to get away.

1. A fast fish with fins out. 2. The fins are in for moving at speed.

they flatten their fins against their bodies, or fold them into grooves or slots. This makes them a better shape to slip through the water easily and speedily.

Next to the Sailfish comes the Marlin which can swim at 80 k.p.h. The Marlin is probably the fastest long-distance swimmer.

5 FASTEST FEATHERS

The fastest living thing is a little bird called the Spine-tailed swift. It could easily overtake most cars and trains. It flies at the amazing speed of 170 k.p.h. It lives in Russia and other countries of Asia. Like most swifts, it spends most of its life in the air. If a swift ever lands on the ground by mistake it may never fly again. This is because its wings are just right for flying very fast, but not much good for taking off from the ground.

Below: Helped by gravity, the Golden Eagle can dive at 290 k.p.h.

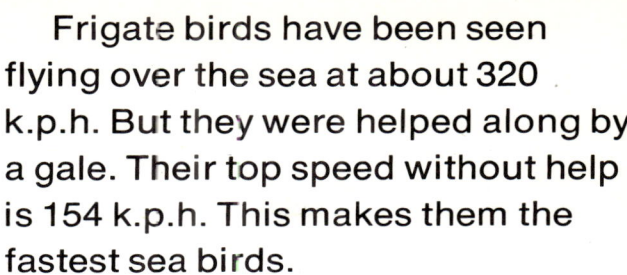

Frigate birds have been seen flying over the sea at about 320 k.p.h. But they were helped along by a gale. Their top speed without help is 154 k.p.h. This makes them the fastest sea birds.

The bird called the Golden Eagle, can dive through the air at 290 k.p.h. But the dive is helped by the force of gravity. But no bird can match the Spine-tailed swift in level flight on a windless day.

Above: Spine-tailed swifts live mostly in the air.

The ostrich is the fastest running bird. This huge creature can scamper along at up to 72 k.p.h. But ostriches are not very good at escaping from hunters, since they usually run around in large circles.

6 INSECTS, SPIDERS AND SNAILS

Above: A Deer bot-fly could not fly at 1,316 k.p.h. as it would burn.

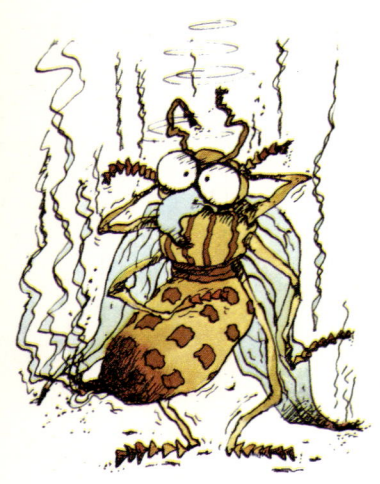

An American scientist once said that the Deer bot-fly was the fastest living creature with a speed of 1,316 k.p.h. Many people believed him, until another scientist worked out that it was not powerful enough to fly at this speed. He also pointed out that it would be burned up by friction, and crushed by air pressure.

In fact the fastest flying insects are the Sphinx moth, the horsefly and the dragonfly. All of these can

Below: Dragonflies are among the fastest flying insects.

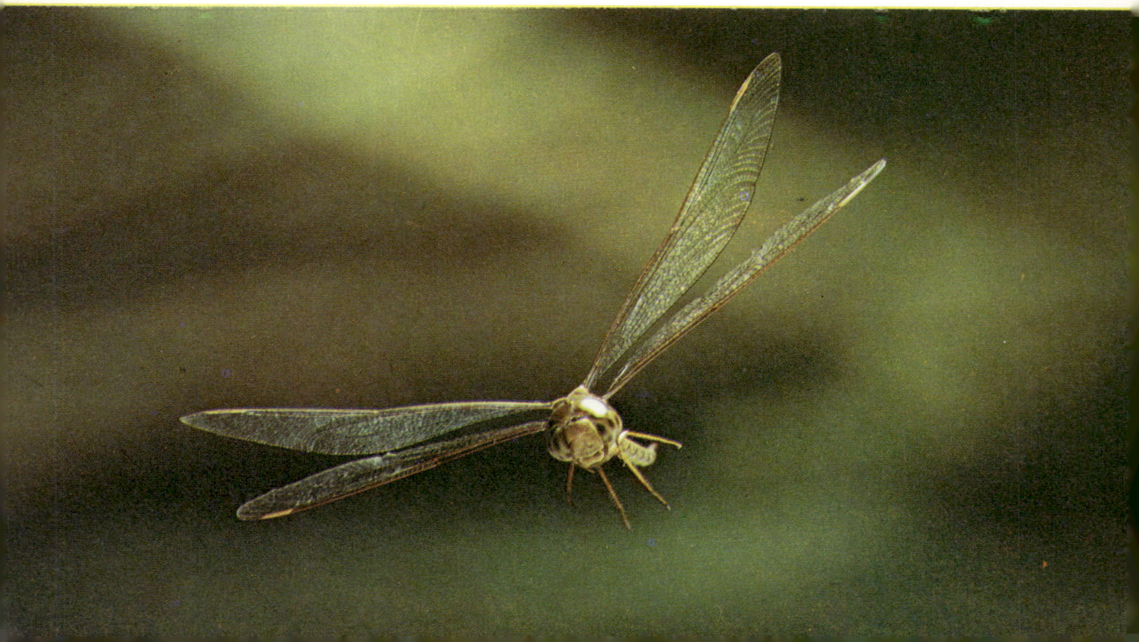

fly at up to about 35 k.p.h. They can fly about twice as fast when they dive and have a wind to help them.

Some insects' wings beat incredibly quickly. One way of measuring this is by the sound of the 'buzz'. The higher the sound, the faster the wings are beating. The tiny midge has the fastest wingbeat known. Its wings make 1,046 beats in one second. That is over four times as rapid as the honey bee's 250 beats a second.

On the ground, the fastest spiders move at around 50 centimetres a second, while the fastest snail can only manage 50 metres an hour.

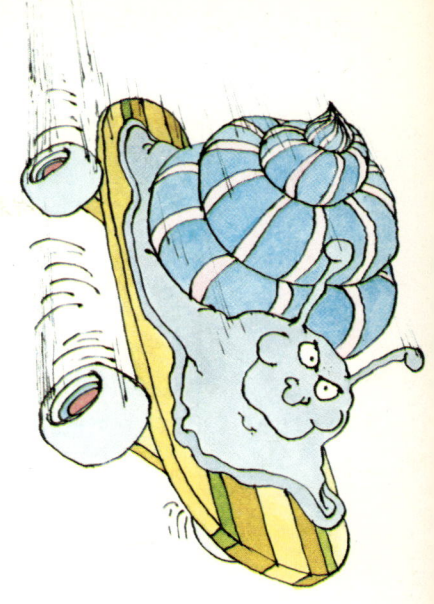

Below: A honey bee buzzes as its wings beat 250 times a second.

7 RAPID GROWERS

Above: The Blue whale not only grows the fastest but is the largest living thing.

The Blue whale grows faster than any other living thing. It is also the largest and heaviest animal in the world. The fertilized egg of the whale weighs just under one milligramme. Yet when the whale is one year old, it weighs as much as 26 tonnes. Its weight has grown almost 30,000 million times.

In the world of plants, bamboo is the fastest grower. Some kinds reach a height of 30 metres in under three months, and may grow as much as 910 millimetres in one day. That is 38 millimetres each hour. The tip of the minute hand on a watch travels round at about the same

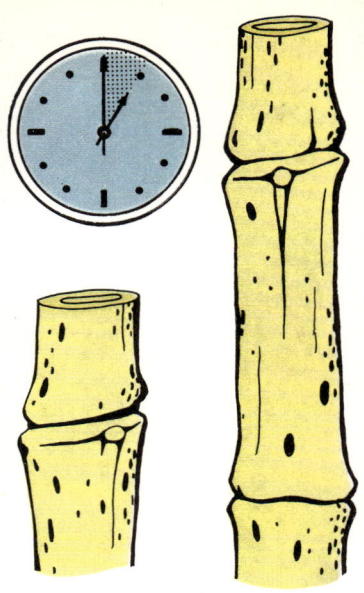

Above: Bamboo grows upwards 38 millimetres in each hour.

Above: Some bamboo grows to 30 metres. The stems have many uses.

speed that the hollow bamboo stem grows upwards.

The insect-eating Streaked tenrec, comes from Madagascar. It is 18 centimetres long and looks rather like a hedgehog. It grows up from a baby faster than any other animal. It stops drinking its mother's milk when it is only five days old. It is ready to have babies of its own at the age of three to four weeks.

Left: Streaked tenrecs take only four weeks to become adults.

8 HOW FAST IS IT?

When you cough you force air out at up to 550 k.p.h. Some experts think that in a sneeze droplets are shot from your nose faster than the speed of sound (which is about 1,065 k.p.h.). This is many times faster than the fastest surface wind, which was recorded on Mount Washington in America in 1934. It blew at a speed of 371 k.p.h.

A bullet shot from a rifle leaves the gun at about 2,500 k.p.h. With

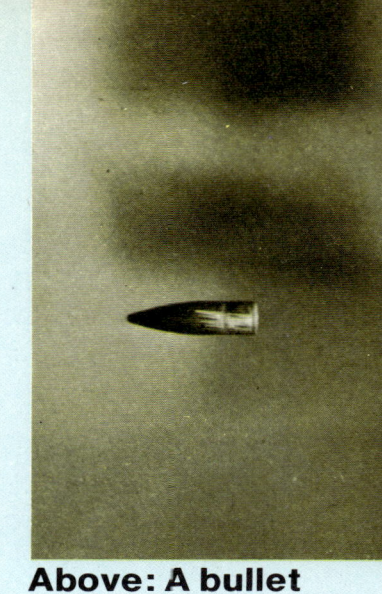

Above: A bullet rips through a playing card at 2,500 k.p.h.

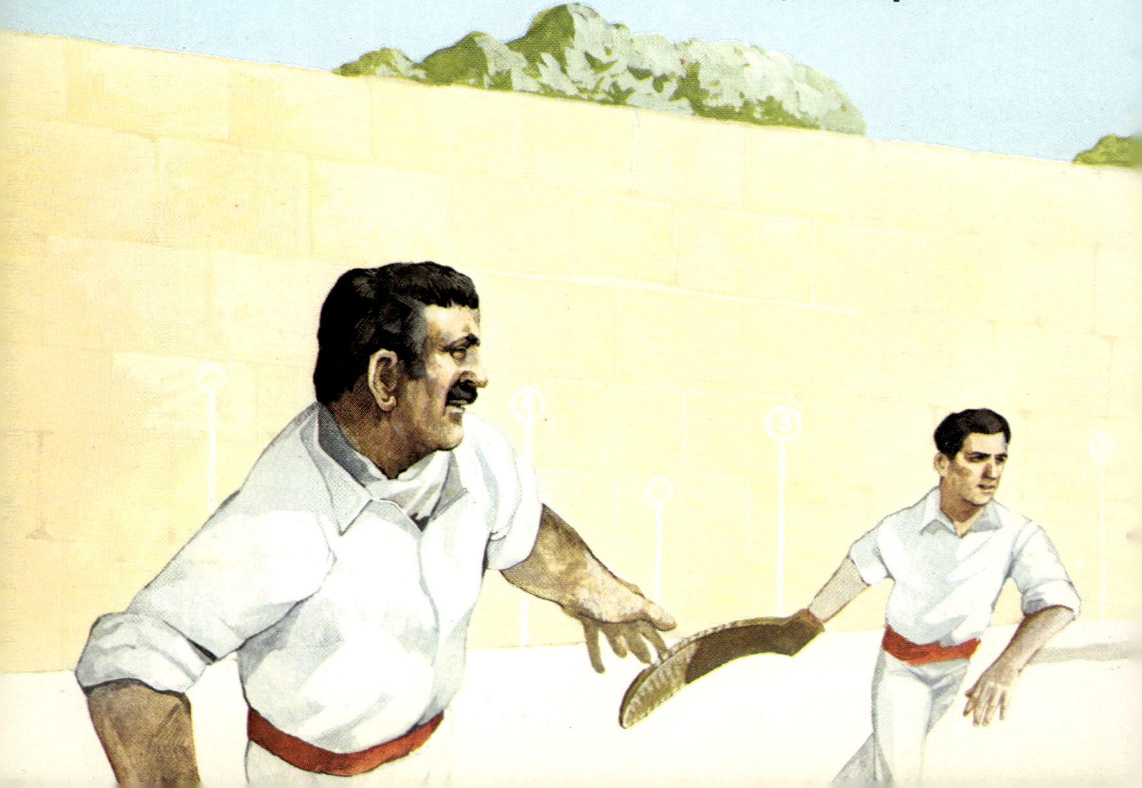

some weapons the speed is over 10,000 k.p.h. An arrow fired from a modern long bow sets off at about 235 k.p.h. Not quite as fast as a golf ball, which when hit by a good player begins its journey at a speed of up to 273 k.p.h.

The fastest ball game is a kind of handball played in Spain and France, and called pelota. One player hurls the small hard ball against a wall, and the other player has to catch it and hurl it back. The ball travels at up to 260 k.p.h.

In cricket the fastest bowlers deliver the ball at up to 150 k.p.h. In ice hockey the 'puck' can travel as fast as 190 k.p.h. and the players skate at up to 47 k.p.h.

Below: The fastest ball game in the world is pelota. The ball is very hard.

9 FASTEST OF ALL

The fastest thing of all, and one of the most mysterious, is light. It travels at 300,000 kilometres a second. Light from the Moon takes just over one and a half seconds to reach us on Earth.

One strange fact about light is that it travels at the same speed in all conditions. If you fire a bullet from a moving rocket, the rocket helps it along. Its speed becomes the same as its own speed plus that of the rocket. But the light shining ahead of

Below: Until we can travel at the speed of light we will never reach the stars in the sky.

Above: A Vandergraff generator is part of an atom smasher.

a rocket travels at the same constant speed as if beamed from Earth.

Two other odd facts are that, one: it seems to be impossible to make anything move as fast as light, and two: very strange things begin to happen the nearer you get to the speed of light. For example, you could shrink or become enormously heavy, and time slows down.

Scientists test ideas like these with giant machines called atom smashers or particle accelerators. These speed up minute particles of matter inside the atom, called protons, until they are moving almost as fast as light.

Right: Travelling at the speed of light might make you very heavy.

Some of the first train passengers.

10 SPEED ON RAILS

The first people to go on railway trains were very excited, and a little frightened. Until then the fastest way of travelling was on horseback, at a top speed of about 55 k.p.h. Passengers soon got used to trains, and they wanted to go faster and faster. The train record speed rose from 95 k.p.h. in 1830 to 144 k.p.h. in 1890, and to 210 k.p.h. in 1903.

Above: Aérotrain is the fastest train in the world.

The fastest speed ever reached by a steam locomotive was 202 k.p.h. by the Mallard in 1938. In 1955 the fastest electric train record was set at 330.9 k.p.h. The fastest train of all is the French Aérotrain. It reached 378 k.p.h. in 1967. It sped along a concrete rail on a cushion of air, like a hovercraft. It was propelled by aeroplane jet engines.

The fastest, as well as the busiest, ordinary railway in the world is the New Tokaido Line. It is in Japan and is 638 kilometres long. Super expresses, called Bullets, streak along at 255 k.p.h. carrying passengers non-stop from Tokyo to Nagoya in only two hours.

Below: The Mallard sped along faster than any other steam train in the world.

Below: A Bullet express about to whisk passengers off at 255 k.p.h.

Above: The S.S. United States.

11 FASTEST WATER CRAFT

1 Hovercraft

Hydrofoil
2

3

Some ships sit in the water, some skim along the surface, and others 'fly' just above the water. Ordinary ships cannot travel very fast. Water is 800 times as thick as air, and moving through it is very hard work. The United States, the fastest passenger liner ever built, had a top speed of 77 k.p.h.

1. Hovercraft move along on a cushion of air. 2. Hydrofoils build up speed. 3. Then they rise above the surface of the water on their foils.

Flying ships, or hydrofoils and hovercraft travel at 150 k.p.h. Hydrofoils 'fly' on underwater wings, which lift the body of the boat right out of the water. Hovercraft skim just above the waves on a 'cushion' of air. Powerful fans blow air down underneath the 'ship' to make the cushion, and aeroplane propellers push the craft along. Both kinds of flying ship are used as ferryboats.

Speedboats which skim along the top of the water are fastest of all. The word record is held by Donald Malcolm Campbell. In 1967 he reached an amazing speed of 527 k.p.h. before his jet-engined Bluebird broke up and killed him.

Above: Donald Campbell in his jet-engined boat, Bluebird.

Below: This hovercraft is used as a ferryboat.

12 SAILING ALONG

Most of the sails on large sailing ships such as galleons and clippers were square sails. These were set across the ship. They worked best in a wind which blew from behind on the sails, pushing the boat along.

Most sailing boats today have fore-and-aft sails. These are set along the length of the boat, and they work like an aeroplane wing. But since the 'wing' is standing on its 'end', it moves the boat forwards, instead of lifting it up. Wind blowing from the side flows over the sail.

Wind from the side pushes a boat forward.

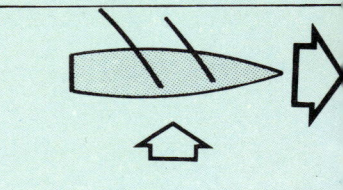

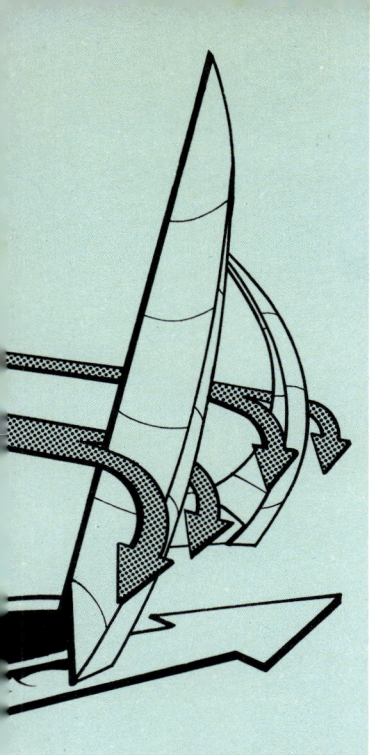

Above: The British boat Crossbow.

Left: Wind blows from the side and flows over the sails set along the length of the boat. This makes a sucking force in front and a pushing force behind the sails and the boat moves forward.

Below: The Cutty Sark, a famous clipper, had square sails.

This causes a sucking force in front of the sail, and a pushing force behind, so the boat moves forward.

With square sails a boat cannot move faster than the wind. Clippers were the fastest sailing ships with square sails and they could reach 40 k.p.h. But a boat with fore-and-aft sails can sail much faster than the wind. In 1975 the British racing boat Crossbow became the first sailing boat to sail faster than 30 knots—her speed was 57 k.p.h.

Wogglebug, a steam car, was the fastest vehicle in 1907.

13 QUICKEST CARS

Only once has a car been the fastest vehicle on Earth—on 26 January 1907. The car's name was Wogglebug, and it had a steam engine. Racing along the sand on a beach in Florida, America, Wogglebug reached 241 k.p.h. It then hit some ridges in the sand, spun over, and broke up. The driver was thrown out, but amazingly he was not badly hurt.

Before Wogglebug, trains were faster than cars. After Wogglebug, aeroplanes and then space craft

Left: The World's fastest jet car is Spirit of America.

were the fastest on Earth.

In Russia and Australia cars are being made that people hope will travel faster than sound. But no car has broken the sound barrier yet. The fastest cars of all are thrust along by rockets or jet engines. The fastest jet car is Spirit of America—Sonic 1, which reached 988 k.p.h. in 1965. The fastest car driven by its wheels was Donald Malcolm Campbell's Bluebird. Its top speed was 716 k.p.h.

Left: Donald Campbell's Bluebird.

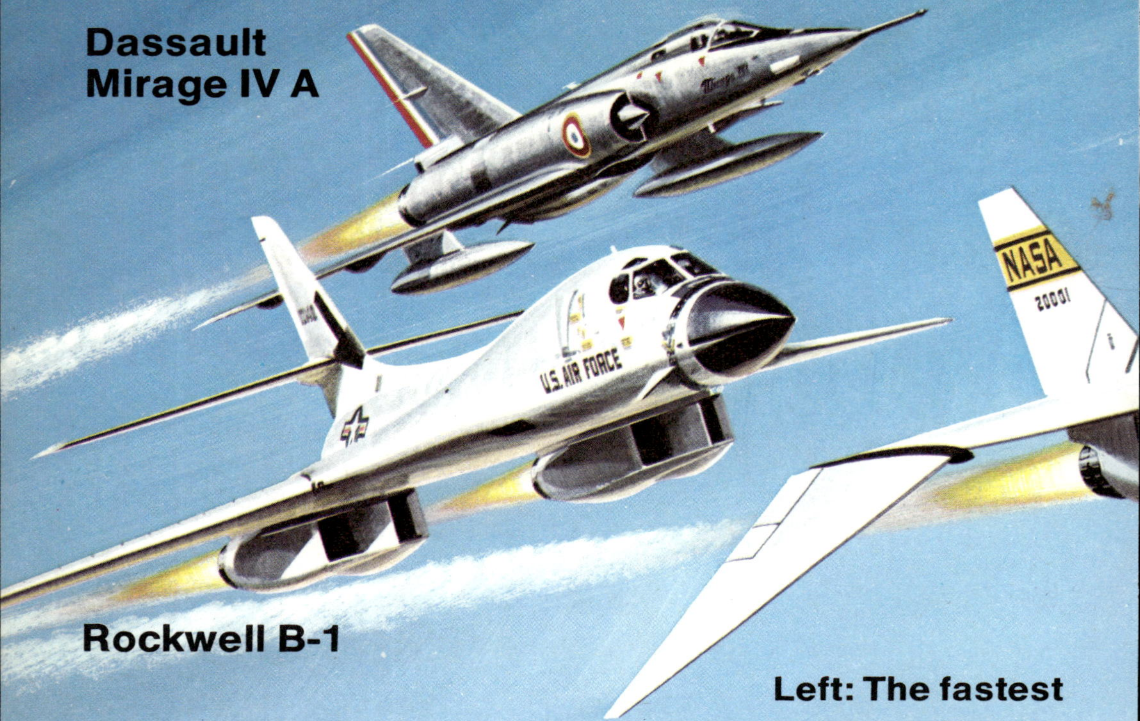
Dassault
Mirage IV A
U.S. AIR FORCE
NASA
20001
Rockwell B-1

Left: The fastest bomber aircraft today fly at about the same speed.

14 SPEED ON THE WING

Just over 25 years ago the world's fastest-ever sea liner, United States, crossed the Atlantic Ocean in three and a half days. Today the fastest airliner, Concorde, does the journey in under three hours. Concorde can travel at up to 2,180 k.p.h. which is over twice the speed of sound. Concorde is also the world's first supersonic passenger airliner used on passenger services. Supersonic means faster than sound.

British airways

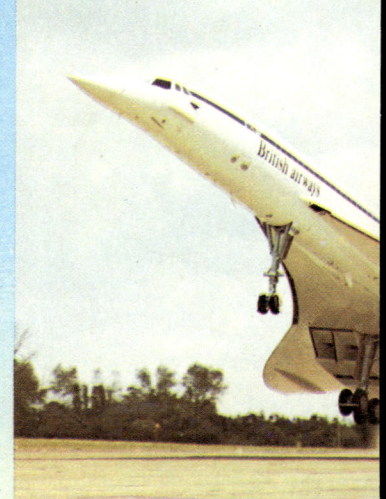

North American XB-70A Valkyrie

Right: The North American XB-70A Valkyrie could fly at 3,220 k.p.h.

Below: Concorde is supersonic.

The fastest bomber aircraft are the French Dassault Mirage IV A, and the American Rockwell B-1. They fly at about the same speed. Before these aircraft there was an even faster bomber, but it is not made any more. It was the North American XB-70A Valkyrie. It had tiny wings near the nose and the tips of its main wings could be folded down. Its top speed was over 3,220 k.p.h. which is over three times the speed of sound.

Smaller jet warplanes fly faster still. Fastest of all is the American Lockheed SR-71. Carrying cameras instead of guns, it flies 24 kilometres above the ground at up to about 3,550 k.p.h. The Russian Foxbat has a top speed of 3,395 k.p.h.

15 ROCKET POWERED

The men who travelled the fastest are the three men who went around the Moon in the Apollo 10 space craft. On 26 May 1969 they reached a record speed of 39,897 k.p.h. as they hurtled back to Earth.

Almost all engines need air. So they do not work in space, where there is no air. A rocket is the only engine that works in space. It carries its own supply of air. It is also the most powerful of all engines.

Blue Flame, the world's fastest

Above: The crew of Apollo 10.

Below: Blue Flame beat all records to be the fastest car.

Above: The fastest vehicle ever made is Pioneer 11.

car, was rocket-powered. Looking more like a rocket than a car, it reached the fantastic speed of 1,046 k.p.h. The fastest aircraft, also rocket-powered, was the North American X-15A-2. After being carried up into the sky by a 'mother plane', it flew at 7,297 k.p.h.

The fastest vehicle ever made is also rocket-powered. This is the space craft Pioneer 11. It was launched from Earth on 5 April 1973. In December 1974 it flew past the planet Jupiter at 173,214 k.p.h.

WORDS YOU MAY NOT KNOW

Clipper   A swift, 19th-century sailing ship.

Fore-and-aft   The fore sail is at the front of a sailing craft and the aft sail is at the back.

Galleon   A type of sailing ship that first appeared in the 16th century.

Gravity   The force from the Earth keeping all things firmly on the surface.

Larva   The stage of an insect's life between the egg and the pupa.

Mysterious   An event or perhaps a person's behaviour which cannot be explained in the ordinary way.

Propelled   Driven or pushed forward.

Scientist   A person who studies science, such as biology, chemistry and physics.

Slipstream   The current of air or water driven backward by a force pushing forward.

Sound barrier   Air resistance at or just above the speed of sound.

Torpedo   Cigar-shaped weapon carrying explosives. It is used to attack enemy ships or submarines.

Vehicle   Anything mechanical that can be used to transport people or goods.

Weapon   An instrument of any kind used to attack an enemy.

Windshield   A screen to protect a pilot or driver from the full force of the wind.